# SERMON OUTLINES ON WOMEN OF THE BIBLE

Charles R. Wood

**KREGEL PUBLICATIONS**
Grand Rapids, Michigan 49501

*Sermon Outlines on Women of the Bible*, by Charles R. Wood. © 1990 by Kregel Publications, a division of Kregel, Inc., P. O. Box 2607, Grand Rapids, MI 49501. All rights reserved.

Cover: Don Ellens

**Library of Congress Cataloging-in-Publication Data**

Wood, Charles R. (Charles Robert), 1933–
Sermon outlines on women of the Bible / Charles R. Wood.
    p.    cm.—(Easy-to-use sermon outline series)

1. Women in the Bible—Sermons—Outlines, syllabi, etc. I. Title. II. Series: Wood, Charles R. (Charles Robert), 1933-    . Easy-to-use sermon outline series.

BS575.W63    1990    220.9'.2'082—dc20    90-37992
                                          CIP
ISBN    0-8254-3989-2  (pbk.)

    2 3 4 5 6 Printing/Year 97 96 95 94 93

*Printed in the United States of America*

# Contents

## Textual Index

# Introduction

In a day of renewed interest in and emphasis on the role and function of women in Christian ministry, a series of sermons based on the lives of women in the Bible is both appropriate and relevant. God's dealing with Biblical women and their responses provide a basis from which principles may be derived that will undergird the formation of a philosophical position.

A surprisingly large number of women are included in the biblical record, and their lives run the full gamut from the guileless innocency of the Virgin Mary to the studied perversity of Ahab's Queen Jezebel. It is interesting that some of the more instructive biblical women remain unnamed, but are rather known by their exploits, accomplishments, and commitments.

With the exception of five outlines specifically derived from sermons in Spurgeon's *The Treasury of the Bible*, all the material in this book has either been prepared by the compiler and preached in his own pulpit or prepared and taught by his wife in the course of her ministry to women. All the outlines have been carefully revised for publication with a specific attempt made to make the material readily usable.

Here is material for a variety of uses. A series of messages on "Great Women of the Bible" could easily be prepared by a process of personal selection; a specific outline could produce a talk for a women's group; a mother-daughter banquet speaker might find the ideal message; and the leader of a ladies' Bible study would have material to structure several months of lessons.

This book will prove most helpful if both the outlines and the Scriptures on which it is based are carefully studied prior to any presentation. The vast majority of the messages are expository in nature, and all of them are designed to be intensely practical in application.

The fact that a number of women figured prominently in the life of our Lord encourages the compiler of this series to believe that there is benefit to be gained by men and women alike from a consideration of the women who enhance the pages of Scripture. These outlines are put forth with the sincere prayer that the God of the Word may use His Word to bless His church.

# Eve: God's Pattern for Woman

### Genesis 1:26, 27; 2:7, 18-25; 3:1-13, 16-21; 4:1-8

## Introduction

Much being written and taught today about the purpose and function of woman. There is an urgent need to return to the teaching of Scripture for this information. The Bible makes many things clear and plain concerning Eve, the prototype woman.

I. **Eve: A Woman by Creation**
   A. God made her as part of man.
      1. Made her from Adam without causing him pain.
      2. She came from a place near the heart, not near the head or the foot.
   B. They were to have an abiding union.
   C. Eve and her descendants were to be loved, protected and provided for.
   D. She had everything going for her.

II. **Eve: A Woman by Purpose**
   A. She was to "complete" Adam.
      1. She was something he was not, something he could not be.
      2. She was the "good thing" which Adam lacked.
   B. She was to be a help suited ("meet") to him.
   C. She was to be led and taught by him.
      1. She failed in the garden because she did not seek his leadership.
      2. She failed because he had not properly taught her (she knew the facts but not the real truth).
   D. She was to obey him (Gen. 3:16).

III. **Eve: A Woman in Action**
   A. She walked with her husband.
   B. She was taught household skills by God (such as sewing).
   C. She bore Adam's children.
      1. "Eve" means life.
      2. Mother of all living.
   D. She apparently kept the home while Adam tilled the ground.

IV. **Eve: A Woman in Failure**
   A. She bears no more responsibility for their sin than Adam, but she did lead in it.
   B. She started out fulfilling all God's purposes.
      1. She failed God.
      2. Thus she failed in each of her roles.

C. By exalting her own opinion, Eve usurped authority over the Word of God (which mankind has continued to do ever since).

## Conclusion

Eve teaches us the importance of placing final authority in God's Word rather than in human opinion.

# Hagar: Victim of Horrible Circumstance

## Genesis 16:1-16

**Introduction**

Hagar is the kind of a sad chapter that sometimes occurs in the life of a great man. Abraham had yielded to the unbelief of Sarah; in the process, he had created all kinds of present and future problems. Hagar was trapped in the midst of all the confusion.

I.   **The Setting**
  A.   God had promised Abraham that he would be head of a great nation.
  B.   At age 75 Abraham began to put God's program into practice, and he was reassured of God's great promise of posterity.
  C.   Abraham and Sarah had no children.
    1.   The years continued to pass.
    2.   Sarah became nervous about God's promise.
  D.   Sarah convinced Abraham to take God's will into his own hands.

II.   **The Story**
  A.   Hagar: the innocent bystander.
    1.   She was an Egyptian.
    2.   She lived comfortably in Abraham's home.
    3.   She was one of Sarah's favorites (much younger than her mistress).
  B.   Hagar: the misused.
    1.   Practice of giving maid to husband allowed at time.
    2.   She was thus a "concubine" or second wife.
    3.   Child born to this arrangement would be legal heir.
  C.   Hagar: the victim of circumstances.
    1.   Trouble results from wrong arrangement.
    2.   Hagar and Sarah turn against each other.
    3.   Abraham again abdicates responsibility.
    4.   Hagar flees from bad situation.

III.   **The Supply**
  A.   Hagar heads toward Egypt.
    1.   Place she had come from.
    2.   Troubles sometimes cause us to turn back to our past.
  B.   God saw her in desert.
    1.   Spoke to her as "Sarah's maid".
    2.   God saw her as that —He saw her with no relationship to Abraham.

C. God questions her decision and direction.
  1. She was coming from duty and heading toward danger.
  2. God tells her to return and submit.
D. As result of her obedience, she is given promises.
  1. She recognized who God was.
  2. She knew something of the character of God ("thou God seest me").
E. Ishmael is born.
  1. To Abraham .
  2. Gave Hagar some joy.

## Conclusion

We are sometimes caught in circumstances not of our making. When we are, it is necessary to remember that God knows where we are, God is watching over us, and God will bring things out right in the end. Hagar reveals to us so many truths about how to handle a bad situation.

# Sarah: Compromise and Circumcision
### Genesis 16—17

**Introduction**

When tracing the life of Abraham, one encounters certain prominent issues: faith, fraity, God's covenant, etc. God's covenant looms large and forms the background of this story.

I.   **Abraham's Promise From God**
   A.  Covenant involved many times.
   B.  All conditional on heir.
   C.  Promise had been focused (15:1-4).
      1.  Not to be someone from his household.
      2.  To be someone out of his own loins.

II.  **Abraham's Problem**
   A.  Promise had been postponed—prolonged (natural problems).
   B.  Breakdown of faith.
      1.  What transpired could not have happened had faith not broken down.
      2.  Human fraility shows up—impatience and self-action.

III. **Sarah's Proposal**
   A.  Her plan.
      1.  Customarily the maid's personal property bound to will of owner.
      2.  Would appear to fulfill condition of promise (15:4).
   B.  Motive probably good but sin involved.
      1.  Double sin.
         a.  Clashed with monogamy—God's will.
         b.  Human devices to bolster divine purposes.
      2.  Steps of sin's outworking.
         a.  Sarah's judgment impaired by bitter feelings (16:2).
         b.  Sarah blames Abraham for her own suggestion (v. 5).
         c.  Calls upon God to judge her self-created mess (v. 5)
         d.  Acts with meanness toward Hagar.
      3.  Sarah gave up so much in the process (v. 3).
         a.  Polygamy—mother of envy, jealousy, and strife.
         b.  Causes Hagar to despise Sarah.
         c.  Sin shows everyone in a bad light.
            (1) Abraham washes his hands of whole thing.
            (2) Sarah treats Hagar poorly.

(3) Hagar puffs up with improper pride.

## IV. Hagar's Flight

A. Flees from Sarah's harsh treatment.
   1. Do not know how severe.
   2. Remember Hagar's haughtiness.
B. Is given an interview with the angel of Lord.
   1. Reminds her that she is "out of place" (v. 8).
   2. Tells her to correct existing wrong of self-will (v. 9).
   3. Gives her three-fold message.
      a. Son.
      b. Name: Ishmael— "God hears" (reminder of this event).
      c. Description of son's character (v. 12) —still true today.
C. Responds to interview.
   1. "The God who sees me."
   2. *Beer-lahai-roi*— "Place of the God who sees and hears."
   3. Returns to her original place as commanded.

## V. God's Provision (v. 17)

A. Covenant reaffirmed.
   1. Revelation of God —*El Shadai*— The all sufficient—able to overcome and subdue nature —the message he needed.
   2. Commandment of God (v. 1).
      a. A God-conscious life ("Walk before me").
      b. Careful attention to details ("Be thou perfect").
B. Circumcision instituted.
   1. A sign of covenant.
   2. Purification right at source of life.
C. Promise of Isaac.
D. Promise for Ishmael.

## Conclusion

Do the will of God. Be patient for God. Keep faith in God. Remember the compassion of God.

# Remember Lot's Wife

## Luke 17:32

### Introduction

Lot's wife was his "worse-half." She was unable to tear herself away from the world, and in a time of trouble, revealed her true character. She shows us that the love of the world is death. Remember Lot's wife.

I.   **Remember That She Was Lot's Wife**
   A.   For all his faults, he was a righteous man.
      1.   She was united to him in the closest possible way.
      2.   She had shared his journeys, adventures and trials.
      3.   She had shared in her husband's privileges.
      4.   She had shared in—and might have learned from—her husband's errors.
      5.   She had likely contributed heavily to her husband's downfall.
   B.   Thus she was a woman who was not without spiritual background.

II.  **Remember That She Had Gone Some Distance Toward Salvation**
   A.   She believed the message that had come about the doom of the city.
   B.   She had actually left the city.
   C.   She is typical of many who go a long way toward Christ and still perish.

III. **Remember That She Did Actually Perish Through Sin**
   A.   She lingered behind.
   B.   She disbelieved what she had been told.
   C.   She dared to look—an act of deliberate rebellion.
   D.   She showed the power of the pull of the world.

IV.  **Remember That Her Doom Was Terrible**
   A.   Her doom befell her at the very gates of the city.
   B.   Her doom came upon her very suddenly.
   C.   Her doom came upon her when she was in the very act of sin.
   D.  Her doom was somewhat the result of her husband.
      1.   When one walks with God and imitates God, one becomes a person of great character (Abraham).
      2.   When one walks with a great man and imitates him, one will always have a weakness of character (Lot).
      3.   When one walks with a man of weak character and imitates him, one will be a failure (Lot's wife).

## Conclusion

Lot's wife becomes a tragic example of the pull of the world and the danger of yielding to that pull. She had a horrible fate because she was drawn two ways.

—Adapted from C.H. Spurgeon

# Rebekah: The Anatomy of Deceit
## Genesis 24—27

**Introduction**

Isaac was the divinely provided son of a special man, making him "extra-special." God had also specially chosen his wife, and all was well until conflict developed over their sons. Then deceit reared its ugly head.

I. **The Beginning of Deceit**
   - A. Isaac evidently was not a strong leader in his own home.
     1. Rebekah played to his weakness rather than his strength.
     2. Obvious that minor deceptions were commonplace.
   - B. Rebekah assisted Jacob in theft of birthright.
   - C. Rebekah interfered in Isaac's plan of blessing (27:1-14).
     1. Hers was a voice of desperation.
     2. Mindful of God's promise, she was not willing to trust God.
        - a. Should have reminded him of God's promises.
        - b. Should have shown him that Easu had actually forfeited the blessing by the lifestyle he maintained.
     3. She took advantage of Isaac's infirmity.
     4. Her deceit not rebuked even yet.
   - D. The second deception (27:41-46).
     1. Everyone should have learned by now.
     2. Shows how one sin often leads to another.

II. **The Fruit of Deceit**
   - A. She influenced another to be deceitful.
     1. Jacob plagued throughout life by lying.
     2. Shows how quickly sinful habits are learned.
   - B. She caused hatred between others.
   - C. She caused many wrongs.
     1. With her help, Jacob learned to cheat by cheating his brother.
     2. With her help, Jacob defrauded his father.
     3. With her help, Jacob was robbed of any sense of satisfaction with his blessing.

III. **The Avoidance of Deceit**
   - A. Since it starts in the heart, heart much be searched.
     1. "The heart is deceitful above all things ..." (Jer. 17:9).
     2. Jesus said that all such things come from the heart.
   - B. There must be a recognition that God will punish it (Ps. 55:23).

C. There must be a realization of the influence it has on others.
D. The heart must be kept in warm fellowship with God.
E. All relationships, etc. must be handled in a biblical way.

## Conclusion

Rebekah got her way, but the results were hardly what she had envisioned. The same effects could have been achieved by doing things God's way. Deceit is always a poor means of getting what one wants.

# Leah: A Tough Life

### Genesis 29—35

**Introduction**

Leah had a very tough and difficult life, but she basically handled her adversity very well. Had she learned one basic principle, she might have left an even better record for us to examine.

I. **Leah Had Serious Problems**
   A. She was the "ugly duckling" sister (Gen. 29:16, 17).
      1. She likely was cross-eyed ("sloe eyed").
      2. Sister was not just average, but actually a beauty.
   B. She was misused by her father (Gen. 29:20-26).
      1. She was married without being given any choice.
      2. She was "pushed off" on a husband who wanted her sister.
   C. She was part of an unfortunate marriage (Gen. 29:27-30).
      1. There was no love involved in the marriage.
      2. She did not have her husband to herself for even one week.
   D. She faced lifelong humiliation (Gen. 29:30; 33:2).
      1. She was always second choice.
      2. She was always "excess baggage".
   E. She had to use her children to gain her husband's acceptance (Gen. 29:31-35).
   F. She was the object of her sister's animosity (Gen. 30:1).
      1. Throughout life.
      2. Especially at times that should have been special to Leah.
   G. She had a very abnormal family situation (Gen. 30:8-9, 14-16, etc.).
      1. Child bearing became competitive.
      2. Had to bargain for husband's affection.
      3. Had to raise her children in abnormal, competitive situation.
      4. Was made to understand that her child-bearing ability was her only worth.
   H. She made her situation worse by succumbing to jealousy (Gen. 30:9-11).
   I. She had to wait most of her lifetime for any retribution.
      1. She outlived her sister (Gen. 35:16-20; 49:31).
      2. Her son, Judah, was in the line of Christ (Matt. 1:2).

II. **Leah Was a Woman Who Learned Some Lessons**
   A. She tried to be content with what she had.

B. She saw her children as her greatest blessing.
C. She obviously developed stronger character than her sister.
   1. No record of deceit or stealing.
   2. She "hung-in" in the face of an intolerable situation.

III. **Leah Was a Woman With a Hurtful Failure**
A. There is no evidence that she called on the God who loved her.
   1. No sign she sought His help.
   2. No sign she sought His salvation.
B. Either she didn't know Him or didn't know how to call upon Him.
C. God would have been to her all that she lacked in life.

IV. **Leah Was a Fairly Typical Woman by Today's Standards**
A. Had an unfortunate family background.
B. Had a less than happy marriage.
C. Lived in the midst of complicated and difficult relationships.
D. Did without things that seemed essential.

## Conclusion
Leah shows the way to make the best out of a bad situation. Her life can teach two important principles:
- I will do what I can to make my situation beneficial.
- I will not waste time blaming others for my situation.

# Miriam: Sweetness Turned Sour

Exodus 2:1-10; 15:20, 21

## Introduction

The Israelites had been in captivity for 400 years. Moses was chosen of God to be their deliverer. Miriam, his sister, was part of his household. Her life is very revealing for us.

I.   **The Experience of Miriam**
   A.   Faithful and responsible (Ex. 2).
      1.   She was probably between ages 7 and 11.
      2.   Showed very good judgment.
      3.   Even then, she was serving her brother.
   B.   A leader of women (Ex. 15).
      1.   First mentioned "prophetess"—a woman inspired of God and directed by Him to know and teach His will.
      2.   She led the women in praising God.
   C.   Defeated by bitterness and strife (Num. 12).
      1.   Was Moses's wife the real problem?
         a.   Miriam may have resented the fact that he had married.
         b.   She was likely spilling out bottled-up bitterness here.
      2.   She was called to assist Moses, not to be his equal or to add to his burden (which she certainly did here).
      3.   She attacked Moses in one of the sore points of his life.
      4.   God did not take her criticism lightly.
         a.   His assistants were to recognize his authority.
         b.   Certainly his own family should have performed better.
      5.   Miriam bore the brunt of the punishment because she was the instigator of the criticism. Now her inner illness was visible for all to see.
      6.   Moses prayed for her healing, and it was granted.

II.  **The Lessons From the Life of Miriam**
   A.   God sometimes uses children to accomplish great purposes.
   B.   Jealousy is a deadly vice.
      1.   "Hostility toward a rival or someone believed to enjoy an advantage".
      2.   Jealousy always ultimately shows itself in action.
   C.   A bitter spirit always has its effects on others.
      1.   Moses was responsible for leading the people to the land.

19

      2. Miriam was responsible for holding them up for a week.
  D. Jealousy must be dealt with, and there are ways to do so.
      1. Recognize it for the sin that it is.
      2. Confess it to God.
      3. Do good to the person toward whom you are jealous.
      4. Try to put yourself in the other person's shoes.
      5. Compare yourself to those below you, not to those above.
      6. Cultivate the habit of perpetual thankfulness.
      7. Try to picture yourself through the eyes of another.

## Conclusion

Miriam was assigned by God with the task of assisting the ministry of her brother Moses. By allowing bitterness to creep into her life, she ended up actually hindering his ministry. She shows us that jealousy is both deadly and something that must be dealt with.

# Jochebed, Mother of Moses
## Exodus 2:1-10

**Introduction**

Her name means "Jehovah is glorious." Her fame lies in her child. Her life reveals a very special woman, marvelously equipped to be mother to a man as great as Moses. Her greatest quality is surely that of faith.

I.  **The Importance of Her Faith**
    A.  She believed Moses to be a special child.
        1.  She saw him as specially related to God's plan.
        2.  She determined that he must live.
    B.  She believed that God would spare him.
        1.  Had no means of making that certain.
        2.  Did what she could to protect him and trusted rest to God.
    C.  She had courage to disobey Pharoah.
        1.  Her motive was obedience to God.
        2.  Obedience to God always ahead of obedience to civil authority.

II.  **The Implemention of Her Faith**
    A.  Faith must be put into action to make a difference.
        1.  Must have been incredibly difficult to keep both the baby and the entire affair quiet.
        2.  Longer it went on, the more her faith must have increased.
    B.  Faith results in action.
        1.  Her growing faith made her inventive.
        2.  Her faith kept her from being paralyzed by problems.
        3.  She must have trained Miriam for her role.
    C.  Faith's reality shows in her works.

III.  **The Issue of Her Faith**
    A.  She threw herself on the care of God.
        1.  Having done all she could, she could then only trust.
        2.  Her trust was well compensated by God's goodness.
    B.  Duty is ours, but events are God's.
        1.  Because of Jochebed's faith, Moses' future was now secure.
        2.  God went even beyond mere deliverance in allowing Jochebed to rear her own child.
        3.  Thus she was able to ground him in God's ways.

IV. **The Impact of Her Faith**
    A. Must have used her time with Moses wisely.
        1. Knew it might be limited.
        2. Was able to overcome pull of heathen culture.
    B. Did excellent job with all her children.
        1. Moses was leader of people.
        2. Aaron was spiritual leader.
        3. Miriam was associated with the leadership of both brothers.
    C. She obviously taught her children.
        1. Faith.
        2. Obedience.
        3. Trust in God.

**Conclusion**

Jochebed shows the extraordinary impact of a godly mother on the lives of her children. Her impact was so great that it was able to overpower all the obstacles to her children becoming what they should. Central to her impact, doubtlessly, was her faith.

# Hannah: The Christian and Her Vows
## 1 Samuel 1:20-28

**Introduction**
The urgency of keeping solemn vows cannot be overstressed.
Hannah provides us an excellent example of this truth.

I.  **The Vow (v. 11)**
    A. The condition.
        1. Man child.
        2. The end of her troubles.
    B. The promise.
        1. Returned for service.
        2. Become a Nazarite.

II. **The Grant (v. 20)**
    A. Hannah's solution.
        1. Comes in answer to prayer.
        2. Her prayer includes the vow.
        3. Complete solution to problem.
    B. God's method.
        1. Uses natural processes.
        2. Economy of the spectacular.

III. **The Crucial Point (vv. 21-23)**
    A. The setting (v. 21).
        1. Time to go up to God's house.
        2. Elkanah questions her.
    B. The intention (v. 22).
        1. Will she take him?
        2. Says she is still going to take him up.
        3. Has full support of Elkanah (v. 23).
    C. The application.
        1. What about your vows?
        2. Crucial time comes after request granted.
            a. God will hold you to it.
            b. Disagreement among two may hinder keeping.

IV. **The Gift (vv. 24-28)**
    A. Hannah keeps her vow.
        1. Religious ceremony.
        2. Explanation to Eli.
        3. Presentation in the temple.
    B. No strings attached.
        1. "Lent" means given.
        2. To stay at God's house for life.

## V. The Reward (2:20, 21)
- A. Outpouring of God's blessing.
  1. God is satisfied
  2. Hannah is satisfied.
- B. Alternative.
  1. Great consequences for failure to perform.
  2. Pharoah a great example.

## Conclusion

Why did Hannah keep her vow? She had a proper concept of the Lord's work, she was sincere when she prayed, she knew the Lord could touch what she had withheld, and she knew this was the only way to blessing and happiness.

What have you promised God? You had better keep your vow!

# Abigail: The Handling of a Difficult Person

## 1 Samuel 25

**Introduction**

Abigail was a gracious woman married to a foolish man. Her handling of the situation when her husband challenged David is a study in how to handle the difficult people that are present in all our lives.

I.   **The Problem Created by Nabal**
 A.  His name means "a fool."
  1. He was churlish and rude.
  2. He was asking for trouble with David.
 B.  David's request was legitimate.
  1. Nabal would recognize the right of none to share in his wealth.
  2. Nabal failed to realize that all he had had come from God.
 C.  David's response was unfortunate.
  1. Did not return good for evil in this place.
  2. Forms significant contrast with his handling of Saul.

II.  **The Solution Proposed by Abigail**
 A.  She was the opposite of her husband.
  1. She was mature and stable.
  2. She moved quickly to act in response to David's request.
 B.  She was humble.
  1. She sought forgiveness.
  2. She honored David.
  3. She did not agree with her husband, but she was willing to take the blame for things he had done.
   a. She sought to make things right with a humble spirit.
   b. What she did was right because done in defense of her family.
 C.  She cast her lot with the man of God.
 D.  She acted in a gracious manner.
  1. Didn't get hysterical.
  2. Didn't seek to blame others.
  3. Likely she could calm David because she had often calmed Nabal.

III. **The Acceptance Provided by David**
 A.  David saw her as a messenger of God.
  1. He listened to her.

2.   He allowed God to avenge.
   B.   David thus spared the one who would become his wife at a later time.
   C.   David allowed her calm to affect him positively.

## IV.   The Lessons Taught by the Story
   A.   Do right no matter how difficult the situation may be.
   B.   Allow your spirit and character to mature.
   C.   Recognize God's hand in your life.
   D.   Recognize the important part you have in the life of others.
   E.   Realize that things will not always be as bad as they are. God will step in and bring deliverance.
   F.   Allow God to use you in the midst of adversity.

## Conclusion

You may never change a difficult person, but think what you can do for yourself. Abigail was unable to change Nabal but she did right by him, David, and by herself as well. She provides a lesson in the constructive handling of difficult people.

# The Witch at Endor: A Soul Sold to Satan
## 1 Samuel 28

**Introduction**

Saul has been out of the picture for several chapters, but he now re-enters the scene dramatically. This is one of the more interesting, controversial, and frightening stories in all the Scripture. It is as if one were telling a ghost story; in fact, it should frighten us a great deal more.

I.   **The Story**
  A.  The approach (vv. 4-8*a*).
      1.  Philistines encamped against Israel—great numbers.
      2.  Saul seeks information from God but can not get it through available means.
      3.  Disguises himself and goes another route.
  B.  The appeal (8*b*-11).
      1.  He asks her help.
      2.  She refuses—fearing trap?
      3.  He promises her safety (note mention of Lord).
      4.  He makes specific request.
          a.  What he can not get from the Lord.
          b.  Has no real need for the information.
  C.  The apparition (vv. 12-14).
      1.  Only the woman sees anything.
      2.  She appears surprised—not used to seeing?
      3.  Saul is revealed—he repeats his promise (finally keeps one).
  D.  The announcement (vv. 15-19).
      1.  Saul's sad state revealed.
      2.  Samuel reviews how he got into the mess.
      3.  Samuel gives desired information (which is not then desired).
  E.  The aftermath (vv. 20-25).
      1.  Saul overwhelmed by information.
      2.  The woman and Saul's servants minister to him.
      3.  Saul goes his way and keeps his promise.

II.  **The Problem: What actually happened here?**
  A.  Witch faked the whole thing.
      1.  Was accustomed to doing so.
      2.  Knew Saul was coming or who he was.
      3.  Knew God's sentence—got even for what He had done to other witches.
      4.  Really doesn't fit details of passage.

B. The witch actually brought Samuel up.
   1. Clearly language of passage—leaves fewest unanswered questions.
   2. Raises questions: Can the dead come back? Can a witch bring back the dead? Where was Samuel? Would God use something prohibited? (Deut. 18:12).
C. Demon represented himself as Samuel.
   1. Satan has power—Demons take on personality.
   2. Satan would know what God has said about Saul.
   3. Woman thus just working with own crowd.
   4. Not what passage appears to say.
D. With the question, don't miss main thrust of passage: to show just how far a man can fall when he turns his back on God and decides to do things his own way.

III. The Warnings
A. The grave danger of occultism.
   1. Beware of Satan's power.
   2. Recognize Satan's power to counterfeit.
   3. Occultism under condemnation of God and child of God has no business with it.
   4. Christian has no need of occult. We know what we need to know from the Word. Should trust God for the rest.
B. The evil end of rebellion.
   1. There is no sign of repentance in Saul.
   2. He develops perverse curiosity about future.
   3. He begins to unravel mentally.
   4. He can get no answer from God.
   5. Rebellion and witchcraft are connected here as stated in 1 Samuel 15:23.
   6. Not all rebellion ends this way, but most of it heads this way.
C. The danger of being set aside by God.
   1. Saul once good and blessed.
   2. Ends up rejected by God.
   3. New Testament teaching in 1 Corinthians 9:27.

## Conclusion

Stay away from the occult! Beware of your rebellion! Turning against the authority God has placed in your life is clearly turning against God. Beware of being set aside by God because of disobedience.

# Jezebel: The Power of Influence

## 1 Kings 16—21

### Introduction

Most women in Scripture are admirable. Jezebel is one enormous exception to this general rule. She comes through as cold, scheming, ruthless, wicked and every other possible negative. Her sad life teaches some practical truths.

I. **The Sad Story of Jezebel**
  A. The wife of a wicked king (1 Kings 16:28-33).
    1. Already the daughter of a heathen king.
    2. Ahab's marriage to her topped all his other sins.
    3. Her unfortunate influence on Ahab began at once (vv. 31, 32).
  B. The enemy of the servants of the Lord (1 Kings 18:3, 4, 18).
    1. As a non-Jew she should have adopted her husband's religion.
    2. Instead of that, she sustained the prophets of Baal.
      a. In place of the Jewish priests.
      b. At the cost of the Jewish taxpayers.
    3. She persecuted the prophets of God at every opportunity.
  C. The usurper of the power of her husband (1 Kings 19:1, 2).
    1. Left alone, a weak Ahab might have listened to Elijah and turned to God.
    2. Her fearsome influence on Elijah shows her enormous power.
  D. A psychologist of evil influence (1 Kings 21:1-7, 15, 16).
    1. She knew how to control Ahab by playing on his desires.
    2. She despised some laws of God and used others.
    3. She made Ahab responsible for a great atrocity.
  E. Guilty of other violations of God's law.
    1. Continually stirred her husband to evil (1 Kings 21:25).
    2. Stood accused of whoredoms and witchcraft (2 Kings 9:22).
    3. She was the ultimate picture of evil and of insult to God.
  F. Known of God for her evil.
    1. Many predictions made against her (1 Kings 21:23; 2 Kings 9:7, 10).
    2. Her death is a story of God's retributive judgment.

## II. The Negative Factors of Jezebel
A. She was a continual influence for evil.
   1. She caused Ahab to be more evil than he otherwise might have been.
   2. She supported and encouraged him in his wrong desires.
   3. She encouraged him to defy God.
   4. She had goals that were formed without fear of God.
B. She often usurped her husband's place.
   1. She dealt harshly with God's prophets.
   2. She threatened Elijah.
   3. She had Naboth killed on her own.
C. She had no regard for the Lord's anointed.
D. She was devoid of most womanly characteristics (compassion, concern, femininity, etc.).
E. She lived a life of rebellion that grew worse and worse.

## III. The Influence of Jezebel
A. Over her husband.
   1. She influenced by words, wishes, desires, goals.
   2. She influenced openly and covertly.
   3. She influenced away from God.
   4. She got what she asked for but not what she wanted.
B. Over her children.
   1. Her influence did not end with her husband.
   2. Her influence also extended to her children (her daughter married the king of Judah and negatively influenced him).

## Conclusion
Jezebel is not a fit role model for anyone, but she does provide a clear example of the things women should avoid in life. Each woman should examine her heart to see if any of the negatives of Jezebel might be present in her.

# The Prophet's Widow: The Necessity of Need

## 2 Kings 4:1-7

**Introduction**

So many needs! We all have them, and no one is immune. We face them in our churches, and we face them as individuals. If God has everything, why the need? A little widow can show us!

I.  **The Demand**
   A.  Her source of supply had been removed.
      1.  She had depended on her husband.
      2.  She was thrown on her real source—God
   B.  God was working in her life.
      1.  God had used circumstances to bring her to trust Him.
      2.  God had allowed her need in order to meet her need.
      3.  Most of us have never put ourselves in such need that God must come through with Heaven's resources.
   C.  Her demand brought her to the prophet of God.
      1.  She came to Him because He was one who trusted God.
      2.  God has stated His ability and willingness to meet needs.

II.  **The Desperation**
   Note her situation.
   A.  Her desperation removed all trust in former sources.
      1.  As long as she had something else, she would not trust God.
      2.  God creates circumstances to throw us on providence.
   B.  Her desperation made her investigate the secrets of the prophet.
      1.  She saw her situation.
      2.  Prophet saw God's salvation.
   C.  Her desperation brought an admission of inability.
      1.  "I can't" to God is very liberating.
      2.  Miracles built upon admission of inadequacy.
   D.  Her desperation brought an act of blind, obedient faith.
      1.  He said to get vessels—not a few.
      2.  She went and borrowed—not knowing why—just by faith (spirit world never makes sense to natural world).

III.  **The Dependence**
   A. The dependence of the man of God on God.
      1. He saw the source.
      2. He looked into the other world.

B. The dependence of the woman on the man of God.
1. Her faith was weak.
2. She just depended on His faith.

## IV. The Deliverance

A. The power—meeting of God and faith.
1. Her faith put a different set of rules into effect.
2. A demand we cannot supply leads to a desperation we cannot solve which leads to a dependence we cannot substitute which leads to a deliverance we cannot stop.
B. The program—amount of her faith determined deliverance.
1. She set her own quantity. God used what she had.
2. We set our own supply.
3. Size of miracle determined by us.
C. The purpose.
1. Need was met.
2. God is always glorified when the needs of His children are met.
D. The person—God.

## Conclusion

Why do we have needs? Because they bring us to the place where God can do something for us. God is able and willing; we set the limits. What is your need? God wants to meet it!

# The Shunammite Woman
## 2 Kings 4:8-37

**Introduction**

Elisha ministered to the Northern tribes under King Jehoram. Shunem was on the road which ran between Samaria and Mt. Carmel, location of the School of the Prophets, so Elisha likely passed there often. The Shunammite woman became a part of his life.

I. **The Story of the Shunammite**
   A. Her hospitality (vv. 8-10).
      1. "A great woman—in both wealth and heart.
      2. A spiritual woman—she recognized Elisha as a servant of God in days of Baal worship.
      3. She was "given to hospitality"—provided rest, refreshment and provision.
      4. She did her very best—even to remodeling her home for Elisha's comfort and entertainment.
   B. Her reward (vv. 11-17).
      1. Elisha sought to express appreciation.
      2. She had right motives—shown in her answer.
      3. Elisha promised her the true desire of her heart— evidently she had not allowed this lack to ruin or even control her life.
      4. God gave her a greater gift than she had given Elisha.
   C. Her testing (vv. 18-31).
      1. The boy, who was a joy to both parents, was suddenly dead.
      2. Her faith shows up in action.
         a. Sends for Elisha.
         b. Says, "It shall be well".
      3. She went straight to the man of God for help.
   D. Her second reward (vv. 32-37).
      1. This reward more likely related to faith than to hospitality.
      2. Elisha prayed first—sensed need of difficult miracle.
      3. Woman left problem with the prophet.
      4. Thanks given before God's gift of a restored life accepted.
      5. A miracle took place in a guest room.

II. **The Lessons From the Shunammite Woman**
   A. A "cup of cold water" results in two miracles.
      1. All God's children are expected to minister to needs.

2. Service should be rendered as part of our efforts to please Christ and not for rewards.
B. Hospitality is a highly regarded biblical quality.
   1. It is lacking in the church today.
   2. It is a grace that any woman can develop.
C. Faith can see one through the darkest night.
   1. Seek the Lord before seeking human answers.
   2. Trust during any waiting period.

## Conclusion

The Shunammite woman provided hospitality without looking for any return. Her kindness was rewarded with something her heart desired. Thus, she showed the value of hospitality. She then lost the reward but regained it through faith, and thus, showed the importance of trust in God.

# The Queen of Sheba
## 2 Chronicles 9:1-12; Matthew 12:42

**Introduction**

She had heard so much about Solomon that she had to see him for herself. The incident of Solomon's contact with this interesting woman reveals a great deal about earnest inquiry.

I. **Her Inquiring Spirit**
   - A. There were many reasons why she should not come.
     1. She was royalty in her own right.
     2. Her own court was already stored with wisdom.
     3. She had a great distance to come.
     4. She was a stranger and foreigner to Solomon.
     5. She surely already had a religion.
   - B. But she did come.
     1. Doubtlessly at great personal expense.
     2. Even without receiving an invitation.
     3. She sought an object far inferior to what men need to seek today.

II. **Her Thoughtful Inquiry**
   - A. She inquired personally (could have sent someone else).
   - B. She went directly to the primary source of what she wanted to know.
   - C. She told him exactly what it was she wanted to know and why ("She told him all that was in her heart").
   - D. She didn't hesitate to ask him difficult questions.
   - E. She listened carefully to what he told her.
   - F. She observed everything in connection with Solomon.
     1. The house that he had built.
     2. The meat on his table.
     3. The seating of his servants.
     4. The quality of his ministers.
     5. The way he related to the house of the Lord.

III. **Her Inquiry Satisfied**
   - A. She made a "confession of faith" ("It was a true report that I heard in mine own land").
   - B. She made a confession of unbelief (". . . I believed not . . . until I came, and mine eyes had seen it . . .").
   - C. She declared that her expectations had been exceeded (". . . the one half . . . was not told me . . .").
   - D. She "envied" his servants (" . . . happy are these thy servants . . .").

E. She blessed Solomon's God ("Blessed be the Lord thy God . . .").
F. She gave to Solomon her treasures.
G. She received of Solomon from his royal bounty.
H. She went home satisfied.

## Conclusion

This ancient queen provides us with a fitting analogy of inquiry after Christ. The inquirer who comes as she did, inquiring as she did, will receive what she did.

—Adapted from C. H. Spurgeon

# Lessons From Rahab
## Joshua 2:1-24

**Introduction**

Everything was being readied for the children of Israel's entrance into land. Joshua is about to repeat something from the past, and it all makes a most interesting story.

I. **The Situation**
   A. Beside Jordan.
      1. About to cross.
      2. Crossing will take them into territory of Jericho (fortified city state).
   B. Facing Jericho.
      1. Must conquer it to secure foothold in land.
      2. Decides to find out what's going on in Jericho.

II. **The Story**
   A. Spies sent (v. 1).
   B. Enter Rahab's house—her profession would give them low visibility.
   C. Rahab shelters and protects them (even lies for them, vv. 2-7).
   D. Gives them necessary information (vv. 8-11).
   E. They enter into a pact with Rahab concerning:
      1. Her safety in the time of conquest (vv. 12-14).
      2. The safety of her entire family (vv. 17-21).
   F. Escape from Jericho (vv. 15-17, 22).
   G. Return to Joshua (v. 23).
   H. Bring good report (vast difference from Joshua's contemporaries, v. 24).

III. **The Statement**
   Considering her culture and character, she makes a fantastic statement to them (vv. 9-13).
   A. I know the Lord has given you the land.
   B. Your terror is fallen upon us.
   C. The inhabitants of the land faint because of you.
   D. We have heard about you.
      1. The Lord dried up the waters of the sea.
      2. You destroyed Sihon and Og.
   E. My people have utterly lost courage concerning you.
   F. The Lord your God is *the God* in heaven above and on earth beneath.

IV. **Showcase**
   A. The mercy of God.

1. Anyone could have escaped who had sought to do so.
2. Shows what God can do in a life.
   a. Heathen to believer.
   b. Enemy to helper.
   c. Sinner to saint.
   d. Harlot to princess (married son of prince).
B. An example of standing against one's culture.
   1. Risked everything for her belief.
   2. Showed enormous courage.
   3. Illustrates pilgrim principle.
C. The working quality of saving faith.
   1. She is praised right along with Abraham (Heb. 11:31; James 2:25).
   2. Her faith was strong enough to make her take action.
   3. Her faith caused her to do works that saved her.
D. The manner of salvation.
   1. She had a message and a tangible contact.
   2. Her action was complete.
   3. She was spared from perishing.

## Conclusion

All people have what she had—the message and the tangible contact. You can act on it as she did and be spared, or you can reject it and perish. Do you have that kind of faith that takes risks for God? God can turn any person and situation around.

# Deborah: You Owe Her That

### Judges 4

## Introduction

Male/female relationships are in a maelstrom, but the Bible presents a clear and balanced picture. In a day of expert opinion, we need to go back and find out what God thinks. A famous boxer once said, "Floats like a butterfly, stings like a bee." Deborah personifies that statement. She was sweet, busy, organized and could sting!

I. **The Situation (3:30—4:3)**
   A. General description of period.
      1. 80 years of rest.
      2. Death of Ehud significant.
      3. Children of Israel did evil—they turned from God, and thus He turned away.
   B. Specific problems with Hazor.
      1. Jabin oppressed them.
         a. Longer than previous trouble.
         b. Nearer to them than others.
         c. Natives resenting displacement.
         d. Formerly subject to Israel and designed to be so.
      2. Very serious time of trial.
   C. Role of woman as judge—Deborah serving.
      1. Prophetess by function.
      2. Serving as judge part of general declension of day?

II. **The Summons (vv. 4-7)**
   A. People begin to turn to the Lord.
      1. Probably already distinguished.
      2. Needed a man to head an army.
      3. Gave divine commission.
         a. Go to Mt. Tabor.
         b. Gather an army of 10,000.
         c. Get army from own tribe and neighbor.
      4. Gave divine assurance.
         1. I will draw Jabin near.
         2. I will deliver him to thee.
         3. Don't worry about size and strength.

III. **The Shrinking (v. 8)**
   A. Barak makes response dependent on her.
   B. Some see it as expression of dependence on the divine.
   C. Obviously a shrinking from duty.

1. Note Deborah's response.
   a. "I will surely go."
   b. Journey will not end in honor.
   c. Sisera will be delivered to the hand of a woman.
2. Clearly a rebuke.

## IV. The Shame (vv. 9-24)
A. Events happen exactly as she said.
   1. Complete success in battle.
   2. Jabin and Hazor overthown.
B. But . . .
   1. Barak must share credit with Deborah.
   2. Jael kills Sisera.
   3. There is much shame involved.
      a. He loses credit which was rightly his.
      b. Woman does and is credited for what man should have done.
C. The heart of the issue.
   1. Barak hid behind a woman.
   2. Failed to provide leadership.

## V. The Significance
A. See here a major problem of today.
B. We debate roles but men surely to lead.
   1. Spiritually.
   2. Physically.
   3. Emotionally.
   4. Mentally.
C. Many men fail to pay what they owe.
   1. Women lead.
   2. Often comes out right.
   3. It is a shame and loss of blessing for the man.

## Conclusion
Are you the leader or are you a Barak?

# Naomi: How's That for a Mother-in-law?

## Ruth

**Introduction**

Naomi's husband was dead, but she lived on in the land of Moab with her family until tragedy struck in the form of the deaths of her sons. Now there was little to hold her in Moab. When she heard the famine in Israel had ended, she decided to head back. Her daughter-in-law insisted on going with her, and the story reveals the stature of Naomi.

I.  **Noami Was a Woman Who Was Concerned With the Welfare of Others**
    A.  Shown as she desires her daughters-in-law to stay behind as she returns (1:8, 9).
    B.  Shown as she further remonstrates with them (1:10-13).
        1.  Cultural thing regarding remarriage.
        2.  Trying to point out folly - they might remarry at home (v. 1:9).
    C.  Shown by her statement in 1:13—"for your sakes."
    D.  Shown by her reaction in 2:19 (this comes after Ruth's success gleaning in Boaz's field).
    E.  Shown in whole tone of book.

II.  **Naomi Was a Woman Who Was Able to Face Herself Squarely**
    A.  Shown as she admits that God's hand is against her (1:13).
    B.  Shown as she accepts a change of name (self-suggested) (1:20).
    C.  Shown as she admits that she has done wrong (1:21).
        1.  Trip into Maob was wrong in first place.
        2.  Likely her suggestion.
        3.  Strong language shows her part in it was being chastened of the Lord.
    D.  Shown in the very fact that she was able to admit wrong and come home again.

III.  **Naomi Was Quick to Recognize the Operation of God in Life**
    A.  Shown by her statements to the two girls when she speaks of leaving (1:8, 9).
    B.  Shown as she admits her wrong (1:20, 21).
    C.  Shown in her reaction to Ruth's coming into the fields of Boaz.
        1.  Knows it is more than circumstance.
        2.  Shows thanksgiving to the Lord (2:20).

## IV. Naomi Was a Woman of Practical Action
  A. Shown in returning to Bethlehem when plenty developed.
  B. Actually shown in going to Moab in the first place even though this action was wrong.
  C. Shown in the way in which she suggests Ruth approach Boaz (3:1-6, 19).
    1. Was acting according to custom.
    2. Was representing the relationship which already existed and which she wished to exist more.

## V. Naomi Was a Woman of Great Faith
  A. Shown by her frequent references to God.
  B. Shown by Ruth's speech.
    1. Frequent and free mention of God.
    2. Ruth could have come back to Bethlehem without accepting Naomi's God.
    3. Such an impression had been made that Ruth wanted the same God for herself
  C. Shown by tenor of whole book.

## Conclusion
Is this the kind of mother you are or will be? You can be by God's grace, but you must first take the last item considered first and that will make the others possible.

# Ruth: Deciding for God
## Ruth 1:16

**Introduction**

Ruth's decision to stay with her mother-in-law and to return to Israel with her was a unique act on the part of a special young woman. That decision has a great deal to teach us about deciding for God.

I.   **Affection for the Godly Should Influence Us to Godliness**
     A.  Ruth was influenced for God by her love for Naomi.
         1.  There was the influence of companionship.
         2.  There was the influence of admiration.
         3.  There was the influence of instruction.
     B.  Ruth loved Naomi so much that:
         1.  She desired to cheer and support her by her presence.
         2.  She feared being separated from her.

II.  **Resolves to Godliness Will Be Tested**
     A.  It had been tested by the poverty and sorrow of Naomi.
     B.  It was tested when she was bidden to count the cost.
     C.  It was tested by the apparent coldness of one in whom she trusted.
     D.  It was tested by the departure of her sister-in-law.
     E.  It was tested by the silence of Naomi.

III. **True Godliness Lies in the Choice of God**
     A.  God was Ruth's choicest possession.
     B.  God was Ruth's only instructor.
     C.  God was Ruth's entire trust and stay.

IV.  **Resolves to Godliness Makes Us Choose God's People As Well**
     A.  She chose to identify with her mother-in-law.
     B.  She did so without regard to the opinion of her own people.
     C.  She did so without expectation of receiving much.
     D.  She was rewarded uniquely.

**Conclusion**

There is much to learn from Ruth's decision to follow her mother-in-law's God. May we be as wise in our decisions.

—Adapted from C. H. Spurgeon

# The Samaritan Woman
### John 4:5-38

**Introduction**

The dialogue between Christ and the Samaritan woman is most interesting. He knew her better than she knew herself. The interview reveals much about salvation.

I. **Salvation Is for All**
   A. It is even for a woman, even for women held in low esteem by society.
   B. It is even for a Samaritan woman.
      1. Non-Jews were looked down upon.
      2. Samaritans were viewed as worse than non-Jews.
   C. It is even for a prostitute.
      1. She was certainly immoral.
      2. She was likely professionally so.

II. **Salvation Must Deal With the Problem of Sin**
   A. Christ exposed her real self.
      1. Actually allowed her to expose it.
      2. Got to real heart of matter and matter of heart.
   B. Exposed nature of her true need.
   C. Sin is always the initial problem and must be dealt with.

III. **Salvation Is Spiritual in Essence**
   A. Men try to relate salvation to tangible things.
      1. Good works.
      2. Morality.
      3. Rituals and ceremonies.
   B. Salvation can never be dealt with until the spiritual explored.

IV. **Salvation Changes Lives**
   A. She immediately went looking for others.
   B. In the process, she positionalized herself relative to Christ.
   C. She brought others to Christ.

**Conclusion**

The encounter between Christ and the woman reveals several key issues in salvation as she manifests evidence of having been saved and shows how it happened. There is no other way to salvation!

# Eulogy of a Mother

### Proverbs 31:10-31

**Introduction**

Most can conjure up a memory picture of mother. Whatever yours was like, the Bible paints a picture of an ideal mother in Proverbs 31. This was written in another age; but the principles it propounds remain the same.

I. **The Worth of the Ideal Mother (v. 10)**
   A. Some say, "typical woman"—not so.
   B. Worth is tied to rarity.

II. **The Character of the Ideal Mother (11-19)**
   A. Trustworthy (vv. 11, 12)—finds her full satisfaction in her own husband.
   B. Industrious (vv. 13-19).
      1. Works willingly (v. 13).
      2. Places care of household above own comfort (v. 15).
      3. Strong in her ways (v. 17).
   C. A good provider (vv. 20-22) (Note order).
      1. For others (v. 20).
      2. For her own household (v. 21).
      3. For herself (v. 22).

III. **The Effect of the Ideal Mother (vv. 23-27)**
   A. Her husband's welfare is promoted (vv. 23, 24).
   B. Has personal peace (v. 25).
      1. Clothed with respect and honor.
      2. Has no fear of the future.
   C. Her family prospers under her guidance (vv. 26, 27).
      1. She speaks wisdom.
      2. Her teachings are guided by law of kindness.
      3. Generally oversees with good.

IV. **The Reward of the Ideal Mother (28-31)**
   A. She received the praise of her family (28, 29).
      1. Should be respected anyhow.
      2. This is the most important item of reward—makes her content.
   B. Gets to partake of fruits of own labor (v. 31).

V. **The Secret of the Ideal Mother (v. 30)**
   A. She is not typical.
   B. The pathway is through recognition of spiritual values (v. 31).

1. No woman can hope to be even an adequate wife and mother until she knows the "fear of the Lord."
2. Fear of the Lord is so central (1:7; Eccl. 12:13).

## Conclusion

Everything here is possible for the one who has trusted the Lord, and it can be found in surrendered, close daily fellowship with Him. Every husband and child also has rights, the right to a Christian wife and mother. Is this a portrait of you, Mother? It can be if you will let God have His way in your life.

# Mary of Bethany: She Hath Done What She Could

## Mark 14:3-9

**Introduction**

Not too many get to choose or know their own epitaph. Mary of Bethany knew hers beforehand, and most of us would like the same one, "She hath done what she could." Look at what she did.

I. **The Recitation of Her Act**
   A. An act of boldness.
      1. To act in front of others.
      2. To do something apparently pointless.
      3. You will never do what you can until you get involved in some act of boldness.
   B. An act of blessing.
      1. Spontaneous.
      2. Arose out of gratitude (resurrection of brother and teaching for self).
      3. You will never do what you can do until you do something for Him prompted by sheer love.
   C. An act of bounty.
      1. She gave all of all she had.
      2. She gave the very best and most precious.
      3. You will never do what you can until you give Him both your all and your very best.
   D. An act of brokenness.
      1. Breaking of box (vessel) showed extent of self-sacrifice.
      2. Vessel would never again be used for lesser purpose.
      3. You will never do what you can until you have known brokenness and self-sacrifice.
   E. An act of belief.
      1. Somehow tied in to His crucifixion.
      2. She was showing belief in Him and in what He was doing.
      3. You will never do what you can until you have come to belief in Christ.

II. **The Result of Her Act**
   A. Stinging.
      1. Misunderstanding.
      2. Criticism.
      3. As soon as you do what you can, you can expect this!
   B. Surprising.
      1. Came from disciples.
      2. Most of them entered in.

3. When you start doing what you can, you can expect to hear from God's people.
C. Satanic.
   1. John 12:4 shows real source.
   2. Others followed lead by Judas.
   3. Opposition to doing what you can ultimately comes from Satan.

III. **The Reward of Her Act**
A. Jesus defended her.
   1. He said, "Let her alone. Why trouble her!"
   2. He always defends those who do what they can.
B. Jesus commended her.
   1. She hath wrought a good work on me.
   2. She hath done what she could—ultimate.
   3. Jesus always commends doing what we can.
C. Jesus remembered her.
   1. This which she hath done shall be spoken of her.
   2. Provided perpetual memorial (don't know what some disciples did).
   3. The final memorial—"Well done, thou good and faithful . . ."

**Conclusion**

She hath done what she could! Will it ever be said of you? Not unless there is boldness, blessing, bounty, belief, brokenness. Jesus had some strange things in His treasure house—a widow's mite, some cups of cold water, a broken vase. What does He have of yours?

# Elizabeth: A Woman Chosen of God

## Luke 1:5-25, 36, 39-80

**Introduction**

Elizabeth is known solely in relationship to others. She is a woman of great character (godliness, faith, patience, humility, etc.), and her life has many lessons to teach us.

I.   **Her Preparation for Her Calling**
   A.   Came from godly family line.
      1.   She was a "daughter of Aaron."
      2.   Piety required for wife of priest.
   B.   She walked in God's commandments (v.6).
      1.   Implies a personal relationship with God.
      2.   She did not depend on her husband's spirituality.
      3.   She served God in the spirit of the law rather than in the letter.
   C.   She had accepted God's plan for her life.
      1.   Had not grown embittered by denied expectation.
      2.   Seemed willing for God's will.

II.  **Her Relationship to Mary**
   A.   She hid herself—possible reasons include:
      1.   Awkward situation in which she wished to be left alone.
      2.   Sensed a special spiritual time to be alone with God.
   B.   She was delighted to see Mary.
      1.   They could talk and worship together.
      2.   The joint miracles were a wonderful thing to share.
   C.   She recognized the superiority of Mary's situation from the beginning.
      1.   The action of the Holy Spirit had made that very plain.
      2.   She had been the recipient of a miracle yet could yield to Mary.
   D.   She could rejoice in the blessing of another without any jealousy.

III. **Her Relationship to Zacharias**
   A.   She was a crown to his ministry.
   B.   She does not chide him for his lack of faith.
   C.   She appears to have accepted him as he was.
   D.   She supported him, especially at the time of the naming of the baby when there was family pressure to do differently.
   E.   She shared spiritual interest with him.

IV. **Her Faith in God**
   A. She walked devoutly into older age.
      1. Showed no impatience with God.
      2. Was one of several mothers blessed in waiting (Sarah, Rebekah, Hannah).
   B. She accepted Zacharias's story.
      1. Must have been very difficult to believe.
      2. She shows absolute faith in him.
   C. May explain why God spoke to Zacharias and not to her—her faith may have already been sufficient without further help.

V. **Her Effect on Us**
   A. She teaches us to have faith in God.
   B. She teaches us to wait patiently for God when human resources are exhausted.
   C. She teaches us to give attention to one's own spiritual state (to stay in the place where God can bring blessing).

**Conclusion**

   Elizabeth likely did not live to see John minister. She had the prediction, and her faith made it as if it were reality. We have much to learn from this woman chosen of God.

# She Gave It All She Had (The Widow in the Temple)

## Luke 21:1-4

**Introduction**

Widows never have cut a very striking figure in human society, and things were even worse in the times of Christ. Even a careless and insensitive society wasn't allowed to ignore the excellence and brilliance of one widow. Christ singled her out, and her brief moment in the limelight left behind a rich heritage of teaching because of several things she knew.

I.   **She Knew That Obedience Conditions Love**
- A. Love for Christ is shown by obedience to Him (John 14:15).
  1. We are designed to love Him.
  2. No other way to show love.
- B. Love without obedience is hypocrisy.
  1. Really no love involved when we just say words.
  2. To speak of love while disobeying commandments defines hypocrisy.
- C. Love's quality is related to quantity of obedience.
  1. The more you love, the more you obey (and vice versa).
  2. She loved Him and obeyed His commandment on giving.

II.  **She Knew That Devotion Ignores Proportion**
- A. Proportion involves accounting.
  1. Involves thinking in terms of percentages.
  2. Can lead to preoccupation.
- B. Proportion produces concern.
  1. Can move into legalism.
  2. Can distort values—the largest amount may be an expression of greatest selfishness.
- C. Proportion flies before devotion.
  1. Other factors come into play—need, ability, God's will.
  2. Real devotion gives without concern.

III. **She Knew That Sacrifice Demonstrates Surrender**
- A. Surrender settles issues.
  1. Certain key decisions determine whole courses of actions.
  2. Her action doubtlessly based on prior decision.
- B. Surrender redefines sacrifice.
  1. Sure she wouldn't see it as sacrifice.
  2. Big issues often defused by settled decisions.
- C. Surrender brings satisfaction.

1. Take so much heat out of actions and decisions.
2. Her surrender led to her action and doubtlessly left her satisfied.

## IV. She Knew That Faith Transcends Difficulties
A. Her gift left her destitute.
   1. Take the passage to be literal.
   2. Would face her with real difficulty.
B. Her faith conquered fear.
   1. Did what she felt was right.
   2. Trusted God to overcome in regard to consequences.
C. Her understanding was instructive.
   1. Do what God wants you to do.
   2. Trust Him to work out the difficulties.

## V. She Knew That Response Generates Reward
A. Response reaches the awareness of God.
   1. A two-way doctrine.
   2. God's awareness shown by Christ's.
B. Response brings recognition.
   1. So many others in the scene.
   2. Christ singles her out.
C. Response has its reward.
   1. She received reward of his approval.
   2. Reward may take unexpected form.

## Conclusion
She gave Christ all she had because Christ had all she was. How about you?

# Mary: Behold the Handmaid of the Lord

## Luke 1:26-38

**Introduction**

It is difficult to get a clear picture of Mary, the mother of Jesus. She has been turned into a gaudy, garish, gilt-edged Madonna and invested with rights and privileges which are completely without basis in the Word of God. In the process she has been stripped of anything special, including what the Bible does say. It is possible, however, to get a clear picture of her because the Bible tells us quite a bit about her.

I.  **The Person She Was**

Don't know too much here once we have sorted through the tradition—just hints here and there.

A. She was doubtlessly very young.
   1. Can't know for sure.
   2. Likely little more than a teenager.
B. She was very humble—stands out in everything recorded about her.
C. She surely knew much about the Old Testament because she does not view the message to her as strange.
D. She was a sinner!

II. **The Pressure She Faced**

A. What she was told was extremely difficult to believe.
   1. First that it could happen.
   2. Then that it could happen to her.
B. Problem of reputation and talk.
   1. Imagine the misunderstanding—especially if she told the real story.
   2. Possibility of death entered in.
   3. Could be she left town to escape this difficult situation.
C. The prophecy of Simeon (2:34, 35).
D. The details of Christ's life—she never really did understand Him until after His death.
E. The agony involved for her in His death. It appears she grew increasingly bewildered as time went by.

III. **The Purity She Shows**

A. 1:29 —she does not question the angel about what he says other than to wonder how it could be said to her.
B. 1:34 —actually a question of faith, not will this thing be, but rather, how will it happen (or can it happen).
C. 1:46-56 —she sings a lovely song based on the Old Testament. In the midst of her confusion and upset, she sings (and sings praise to God).

D. 2:19 —Mary demonstrates remarkable wisdom and humility in this response. In spite of the pressure she faced, she comes through with a remarkable purity of spirit and spiritual life.

## IV. The Power She Found

How could she respond to all this in the manner she did? How could she be so accepting of conflicting messages and emotions?

A. Key lies in 1:38.
  1. Behold the "handmaid" of the Lord—one who is servant to—who waits upon for direction.
  2. "Be it unto me according to thy word"—indicates complete agreement with God's will.
B. Key developed.
  1. It was not a subjective thing for her—she didn't know all the details.
  2. Possibility of death entered in.
C. Key applied.
  1. What has happened in our lives has happened and nothing is going to change it. We can accept it or reject it, but we are not going to change it. She accepted it and was blessed.
  2. The will of God as it is revealed in the course of our lives is really not the only thing that is hard to accept. We have great problem with the spoken word which comes to us in the Bible. Her surrender was to the spoken word.

## Conclusion

If we as poor, sinful persons are to handle the pressures which come relative to God's will, we are only going to do so through the power of surrender.

# Mary of Magdala
## Luke 8:1-3

**Introduction**

Few people showed more love and devotion to Christ during His ministry because few people had more to be grateful to Him for than Mary. Mary's life story teaches us crucial things about gratitude.

I.  **Mary Identified**
    A.  In relationship to other Marys in Scripture.
        1.  Mary, mother of Jesus (Luke 1:26, 27).
        2.  Mary of Bethany, sister of Lazarus (John 11:1-3).
        3.  Mary, mother of disciples James and Joses (Matt. 27:56).
        4.  Mary, mother of John Mark (Acts 12:12).
        5.  Mary, a Christian in Rome (Rom. 16:6).
    B.  She had been demon possessed.
        1.  Very common to times of Christ.
        2.  She had been healed of the possession.
        3.  Healing had come through Christ.
    C.  She had become a leader of women.
        1.  Shown as following and ministering to Him (Luke 8:2, 3; Matt. 27:55, 56).
        2.  Usually associated with a group of women.
        3.  She is always identified as the leader.

II. **Mary Instructing**
    The instruction comes from her life.
    A.  Had unique ability to show love.
        1.  She owed Him much.
        2.  She showed it from her heart.
    B.  Showed love in a genuine way.
        1.  Jesus knew her love was sincere.
        2.  This likely explains early post-resurrection appearance to her.
    C.  Her love produced gratitude.
        1.  At the crucifixion (Matt. 27:55, 56).
        2.  At the burial (Matt. 27:61).
        3.  At the resurrection (Matt. 28:1; Mark 16:9-11).
    D.  She seemed most devoted of all to Him at the time of His death.

III. **Mary Imitated**
    A.  She should make me ask, "What has Jesus done for me?"

55

B.  She should make me ask, "How do I show my love and gratitude?"
C.  She should make me ask, "How close will I stay to Him?"

## Conclusion

Mary is a study in love and gratitude. She forces me to reevaluate my love and gratitude. She makes me be very practical—"How will I show my love for Him today?"

## Only a Touch

### Luke 8:43-48

**Introduction**

She had fought her physical problem for years, had tried everything she knew and had exhausted all her resources without receiving any help. If only she could get to Christ.

I.  **A Sick Woman's Need (v. 43)**
    A.  Description.
        1.  Nature: hemorrhage.
        2.  Duration: 12 years.
    B.  Efforts to cure.
        1.  Direction: physicians.
        2.  Spent all she had and had suffered much (Mark 5:26).
    C.  Resulting failure.
        1.  No relief.
        2.  Complete frustration as she worsened (Mark 5:26).
        3.  Here is a woman with a dire need.

II. **A Desperate Heart's Action (v. 44)**
    She evidently hears of Jesus and His power.
    A.  Description.
        1.  The approach: from behind on purpose.
        2.  The touch: she "grabbed" the fringe on garment.
        3.  Implications.
            a.  Considerable supersitition.
            b.  Some faith mixed in with it.
    B.  Result.
        1.  Immediate.
        2.  Simplicity: just a touch.
        3.  Note how God honors the faith even though it is now very small.

III. **A Thorough Healer's Reaction (vv. 45, 46)**
    The story could stop here; she has what she needed.
    A.  His question.
        1.  "Who touched me."
        2.  Reveals knowledge of a special touch.
    B.  Diverting response.
        1.  Peter's intervention.
            a.  Christ had a purpose.
            b.  Peter didn't understand it.
        2.  We are too often guilty of this.
            a.  We intervene in God's dealing.
            b.  We simply don't understand God's purposes.
    C.  A pressing retort reveals His source of knowledge.

IV. **A Good Physician's Treatment**
   A. Identification: voluntary and fearful.
   B. Confession.
      1. Public.
      2. Content: how things were and what things are now.
   C. Reason: why did He make her do this?
      1. Chirst already knew who had touched Him.
      2. Met her need.
         a. Proof of healing for restoration.
         b. Further information needed to know that her spiritual illness was healed.
         c. Needed complete assurance.
      3. An initial witness.
         a. No "secret believer" here.
         b. Desired to see her enjoy new life.
   D. Conclusion.
      1. The new relationship: daughter.
      2. The key issue: faith.
      3. The loving charge: move into peace.

**Conclusion**

Here is a woman with a need. She doesn't even know exactly what her need is, yet Christ meets that need.

You may not even know what your real need is, but He does. Christ leads her to make a public confession for her own sake. You need to do the same.

FAITH IS THE KEY THAT MEETS THE NEED!

# Mary and Martha

## Luke 10:38-42

**Introduction**

Mary and Martha were both excellent ladies, obviously greatly loved of Jesus. As sisters they surely had many similar qualities, but this incident casts them as a study in contrasts.

I. **The Martha Spirit Is the Most Common**
   A. There is a general tendency to make service "showy."
      1. Martha wanted everything just right for Christ.
      2. There was evidently a measure of pride mixed in her motives.
   B. Her spirit often shows in the church.
      1. More concern with form than with substance.
      2. More concern with details than with heart worship.
      3. More concern with activity than with spirituality.
      4. More concern with the shown than with the known.

II. **The Martha Spirit Hampers True Service**
   A. It brings an offering to Christ.
      1. It is the less costly.
      2. Therefore, it is the least acceptable.
   B. It excessively emphasizes self.
      1. She was weary in well-doing.
      2. Her weariness was a result of self-centeredness.
   C. It fancies that it is necessary.
      1. She saw her service as indispensable.
      2. She saw her service as more important than Mary's.
   D. It easily becomes vexatious.
      1. She allowed voluntary service to become a chore.
      2. She domenstrated lack of faith by her attitude.
   E. It gives a bad name to service.
      1. She wants the voluntary aspect removed (she wanted Him to *make* Mary help her).
      2. She got away from the inner soul of service.

III. **The Mary Spirit Is Always to Be Preferred**
   A. It produces the noblest forms of consecration.
      1. She later annointed Christ with precious ointment.
      2. That action was an outgrowth of personal preparation.
   B. It refines the manner of actions.
      1. Martha was so task-oriented that she could not examine her own manner.
      2. Mary was so Master-oriented that she need not

examine her own manner.
- C. It creates orignality of act.
  1. Martha does what anyone can or would do.
  2. Mary later comes up with something special.
- D. It rewards genuine spiritualities.
  1. Martha was interested in what she was doing.
  2. Mary was interested in what she was becomming.

## Conclusion

The contrasts between Mary and Martha are typical of contrasts within the church today. As such, they explain a great deal about us and the effectiveness of our service.

—Adapted from C. H. Spurgeon

# Priscilla: Portrait of a Servant

## 1 Corinthians 16:19

**Introduction**

Priscilla, always identified in connection with her husband, provides an excellent example of a servant's heart. Whatever there was to do, Priscilla was available to do it.

I.  **The Background of the Story**
    A.  Paul on his second missionary journey, made this stop in Corinth.
    B.  Aquila and Priscilla had been living in Rome, but they had come to Corinth when Claudius Caesar had banned all Jews from Rome.
    C.  They had the same trade as Paul.
        1.  Customary for Jews to teach children a trade.
        2.  They both plied the trade.

II.  **The Encounters That Reveal Her Character**
    A.  Acts 18:1-3, 11.
        1.  In Corinth around 53 or 54 A.D.
        2.  They entertained Paul in their home.
    B.  Acts 18:18, 19.
        1.  In Ephesus around 54 A.D.
        2.  They are followers of Paul.
    C.  Acts 18:26.
        1.  Also in Ephesus at same time.
        2.  Provide hospitality and teaching.
    D.  1 Corinthians 16:19.
        1.  In Ephesus at close of Paul's three year residence (59 A.D.).
        2.  The church is meeting in their home.
    E.  Romans 16:3-5.
        1.  In Rome at about 60 A.D.
        2.  Helpers of Paul's ministry—put selves on line
    F.  2 Timothy 4:19
        1.  In Ephesus around 66 A.D.
        2.  Singled out for special mention.

III.  **The Character She Exhibited**
    A.  Faithfulness.
        1.  She is not noted for great talents.
        2.  Her loyalty is always obvious.
        3.  She seems to be one of those people who is "always there" when needed.

B. Involvement.
  1. Provided long-term home for Paul.
  2. Appears to be student of Word—was able to teach others.
  3. Strongly supportive ministry.
C. Commitment (involvement at a price).
  1. Placed life on the line for Paul.
  2. Sacrificed for the advance of his ministry.
  3. Cradled at least one local church.

**Conclusion**

We see a wise, capable woman who served alongside her husband. She exhibits the spirit of a servant. Would Paul's ministry have been what it was without the contribution of Priscilla and Aquila?

# Eunice: Mother of a Preacher
## 2 Timothy 1:5

**Introduction**

She was a devout Jewess who had likely been saved as a result of Paul's earlier ministry. Nothing is known of her husband. She had sought to train her son, Timothy, in godly ways, and she is most known for the impact of her life on that of her son.

I. **She Was a Godly Woman**
   A. She had a reputation for godliness.
      1. Her life had made an impression on the apostle Paul.
      2. She had a very high regard for Scripture.
      3. She knew that godliness leads to responsibility rather than responsibility building godliness.
   B. She sought to train her child(ren) well.

II. **She Knew Significant Spiritual Success**
   A. This success may have come in spite of circumstances in her home.
      1. She was either a widow or the wife of an unbeliever (probably the latter).
      2. She was victorious in a difficult situation.
   B. She proves that it is possible to rear children for God alone or with an unsaved mate.

III. **She Was Willing to Give Her Son to God**
   A. Her situation had likely created a closeness to Timothy.
   B. When God asked for him (through Paul), she was willing to give him up.
      1. He was young, and he was not strong.
      2. She knew his success in life would depend on being used of God.

IV. **She Had Taught Her Son Special Qualities**
   A. He had been taught obedience (1 Tim. 1:1-4, 18).
   B. He had been taught dedication to a hard task (1 Tim. 4:12-16).
   C. He had been taught holy living (1 Tim. 6:11-14, 20).
   D. He had been taught to love and to feel deeply (2 Tim. 1:1-4).
   E. He had been taught to be loyal (2 Tim. 4:9, 10, 21).

**Conclusion**

Eunice shows the impact of a mother as well as the importance of rearing children well and the importance of teaching them good character. The good job Eunice did as a mother accounts for the fact that we know her through the ministry of her preacher son.

# *Titles in the Easy-to-Use Sermon Outline Series*

The busy pastor will find a wealth of "sermon starters" available in these 11 volumes compiled and edited by Charles R. Wood which addresses a variety of subjects.